I'm Not My Star Sign

Sagittarius Edition

Jake Adie

jadie
BOOKS

Published by
Jadie Books Limited 2010

Copyright © Jake Adie 2010

ISBN 978 0 9566102 6 3

Cover illustration by Jake Adie

Typesetting by Jake Adie

Printed & bound by
York Publishing Services Ltd
64 Hallfield Road
Layerthorpe
York
YO31 7ZQ

This book is sold subject to the condition that it shall not, in any circumstances, be lent, resold, hired out or otherwise circulated without the publisher's prior consent in any form of binding or cover other than that in which it is published and without a similar condition including this condition being imposed on the subsequent purchaser.

For those not exactly
starstruck by the
sign language

Other Not Really Titles

I'm Not Really 18 (female edition)
I'm Not Really 18 (male edition)
I'm Not Really 30 (female edition)
I'm Not Really 30 (male edition)
I'm Not Really 40 (female edition)
I'm Not Really 40 (male edition)
I'm Not Really 50 (female edition)
I'm Not Really 50 (male edition)
I'm Not Really 60 (female edition)
I'm Not Really 60 (male edition)
I'm Not Really 70 (female edition)
I'm Not Really 70 (male edition)
I'm Not Really Pregnant
I'm Not Really Getting Married (female edition)
I'm Not Really Getting Married (male edition)
I'm Not Really Moving House
I'm Not Really Retiring
I'm Not Really a Grandmother
I'm Not Really a Grandfather
It's Not Really Christmas
I've Not Really Passed My Test
I'm Not Really a Golfer
I'm Not Really a Rugby Player
I'm Not Really a Cricketer
I'm Not Really a Footballer
I'm Not Really My Star Sign (Aries Edition)
I'm Not Really My Star Sign (Aquaruis Edition)
I'm Not Really My Star Sign (Cancer Edition)
I'm Not Really My Star Sign (Capricorn Edition)
I'm Not Really My Star Sign (Gemini Edition)
I'm Not Really My Star Sign (Leo Edition)
I'm Not Really My Star Sign (Libra Edition)
I'm Not Really My Star Sign (Pisces Edition)
I'm Not Really My Star Sign (Scorpio Edition)
I'm Not Really My Star Sign (Taurus Edition)
I'm Not Really My Star Sign (Virgo Edition)

Me, a Sagittarian?

Well, frankly, and I don't wish to disappoint you, I can't really see how I *can* be. You see, being a Sagittarian means that your whole personality is somehow governed by where the constellation, Sagittarius, happened to be when you were born. But I'm certain that doesn't apply to me because,

I'm Not Really My Star Sign

well, I don't have any means of hooking up, in a mental sense, with far out lumps of inorganic matter. I mean, even if I did, these stars aren't, like, just 'up in the sky'. As in, say, those weather satellites orbiting our planet. You know, those magical bits of kit that cost mega-millions

Me, a Sagittarian?

and check out what's going on up there so that the TV weather man can spoil our plans for the weekend. Well there're plenty of them around, believe me, but have you ever seen one? No, of course you haven't. And it doesn't matter how clear the sky is you're going to need some pretty impressive optical aids to get a glimpse of them. And that's because they're a bloody long way away. But, listen, star constellations aren't a 'bloody long way away'. Well, certainly not in terms that any rational person will be capable of visualizing. No, they're as good as, well, non-existent. Not actually *non*-existent but they might as well be because

Me, a Sagittarian?

no one's ever likely to get within several million lifetimes of them. That's the sort of distance we're talking about. No good counting in miles because these little fellows are so far out we can't even begin to imagine the gap between them and us. A mega, mega, mega gap, that's what. So, tell me, with this sort of time/distance scale, what exactly is it that these virtually non-existent lumps of matter do with themselves to enable them to manipulate my personality? Mmm? Bit far-fetched, eh? Okay, look, I'm prepared to accept there is some kind of connection between these heavenly bodies and planet

I'm Not Really My Star Sign

Earth. Yeah, I'm not a complete idiot. It's obvious, when you think about it, that all the stuff that's floating around in the universe is connected in some way or another. I don't know, gravity possibly? Suppose there must be a force that stops everything just parting company forever. Anyone can see there's some sort of pattern to the whole business. I mean, the sun and the moon must obey some kind of rule otherwise we'd wake up one morning to find one, or both, of them had whizzed off to someplace else. And we don't see that, do we? So there's got to be a system. An arrangement. Call it what you will. A set of

Me, a Sagittarian?

universal laws, yes, that sounds right. A set of universal laws that makes everything kind of interdependent. Yeah? And I imagine that's how I'm supposed to get my head around the idea that these far off chunks of rock determine that I'm going to end up with exceptional organisational skills. Or why I'm likely to show inclinations towards being adventurous. Mmm? Is that what being a Sagittarian is? You reckon? Oh, give me a break, please. Look, if something a zillion, frillion, sprillion Earth miles away can exert a lifelong influence on my teeny-weeny brain cells then why can't all these much, much closer man-made

I'm Not Really My Star Sign

Me, a Sagittarian?

satellitey thingamabobs do the same? I mean, they're an awful lot closer. And if it is gravity then, come on, the gravitational pull of the weather sat has got to be greater than the chunks of faraway floating matter. Hadn't thought of that, had you? If my natural inclinations are governed by lumps of virtual rock then, likewise, had a weather sat been up in the sky at the time of my birth, it, too, would have played some major character developmental role. And I'd end up being brilliant at, for instance, getting weather forecasts wrong. Or, looking uncomfortable and unsure of myself in front of a TV camera. Well, I

Me, a Sagittarian?

have no trouble guessing whether it's going to rain when I go on my hols and no one's ever suggested I'm ideal weather-person material for the telly. So, if it doesn't work with weather sats it ain't gonna work with highly questionable lumps of gaseous rock. And what's more, according to the experts, being a Sagittarian, is supposed to accord me some magical relationship with...

I'm Not Really My Star Sign

Because, and listen to this, each of the 12 zodiac signs, in some magical way, enjoys an inextricable association with one of the four elements (and we're not talking periodic table here). No, we're talking air, fire, water and earth. Pretty basic stuff. Nothing complicated. Until, that is, the astrology fraternity get their mitts on them. Then things become anything but uncomplicated. You see, not being satisfied with a whole host of characteristics being universally attributed to your four week-odd birth date period, they confuse the issue by attaching a three-zodiac-sign-encompassing collection of additional personality

I'm Not Really My Star Sign

traits you should also expect to identify with. Which, if you think about it, casts the net, well, pretty wide. I mean, taking your particular star sign features and amalgamating them with another list of add-ons must give them enough scope to cover any eventuality. Like, who's not going to qualify?

A sort of, one-analysis-fits-all strategy, if you see what I mean. Anyway, my particular cross-zodiacal affiliation is fire. Which presumably means my life is somehow going to be especially affected by the hot stuff. In a sort of personal way, I suppose. In a way that will, I should imagine, be exclusive to those enjoying

I'm Not Really My Star Sign

living under the three, relevant fire signs. Well, I'm no mathematician but even I can do the sums on this one. It's got to be around a quarter of the population, hasn't it? Which computes to around 15 million individuals. Not terribly exclusive when you think about it. Not like being an affiliate member of a private club. Or even having an account with some posh credit card company, eh? More like being a retailer's loyalty card holder. Or a supporter of the Labour party. Okay, maybe that is taking things a little too far. But you get my point, surely. I mean, let's consider a group of one of the remaining three-quarters for a minute: a bunch

Fire

of largely earth-orientated star-signers marooned on a desert island. In the winter. And, huddled together on the bare, cold ground with little to protect their bodies from the icy, prevailing winds, they begin to lose all sense of hope. Then, out of the blue, one of their number stands and announces, "Hey guys, if we could somehow muster up the strength to gather a few armfuls of dead wood there's every chance I could conjure up some of my old boy scout skills and get us a fire going. We'll be warm in no time and ready to face the tasks ahead of us. What do you say?" Well, is the response likely to be: "Don't you realise you're talking to a

Fire

bunch of earth signers, mate? Thank you but no thank you – this cold, hard, frosty earth is just fine." Is this what you'd expect to hear? Or, "You're having a laugh, please. Next, you'll be suggesting you want to cook us a fresh, piping-hot meal. We're perfectly happy with this cold earth thank you very much." Is this more like it? Of course it is. NOT! They're going to want to strike up a pretty quick association with the ex-boy scout, if you ask me. As would the rest of us. I mean, which non-fire-related individuals wouldn't? I can't say I've met anyone who isn't locked into a relationship with it. But, then again, perhaps the astros mean something stronger than a mere orientation. Something more than a means of survival. Like being particularly partial to, say, working with furnaces or being a collector of cigarette lighters. Or, something more remote like, an arsonist – well it takes all types. All right, how do you know all arsonists aren't born under one of the three relevant fire signs? There again, it would rather narrow down the list of culprits. Be very helpful for the country's law enforcers, I should think. Mmm, maybe we should examine these Sagittarian associations more closely and check out the . . .

I'm Not Really My Star Sign

Archer

Not a bad place to start. It's an archer that normally seems to be used to depict Sagittarians isn't it? Well, I say an archer but don't they have that strange, half-horse, half-human creature wielding a bow and arrow? A centaur? Yeah? Where did they get him from? Anyway, as I said, not a bad starting place. Now, that presumably means if you're born sometime between 22nd November and 21st December you're going to relate to this curious mutant chap. Well, how bloody stupid. Just because some ancient Greek geek thought the 19-odd stars that make up the constellation looked like one

I'm Not Really My Star Sign

Archer

of their mythical characters it doesn't mean we'd all have arrived at the same interpretation. And then to suggest that certain centaur-like mannerisms are characteristic of people born at that time of the year is plain daft. Listen, when you get time, take a look at a diagram of the little cluster of stars we're all supposed to agree is a dead-ringer for a horse-shaped, human archer. Yeah? Go on, put the book down for a minute or two and get one up on the internet. I'll wait here for you . . . . . . Right, done that? Okay, what did you see, mm? Exactly! A group of stars that someone has done a join-up-the-dots job on that doesn't look

I'm Not Really My Star Sign

Archer

anything like a horse-shaped, human archer. Try joining the dots up in a different order and you'll get whatever you want. Okay, okay, if I'm to be totally honest, it could be an archer. Only could be, mind you. But then, it could equally be a dozen or more other images. In fact, from one orientation, it looks pretty much like a teddy bear with big, sticky-out legs. Really, take a look for yourself. All right, you might think this is all a bit arbitrary but that's exactly my point. It's all down to the interpreter. But if you look at what the astro-crowd read into their accepted archer shape you're likely to come across associations like,

Archer

outdoor activities, aims high, sporty, archery (surprise, surprise) etc. All a bit centaur-like, don't you think? All very convenient, if you ask me. Well, imagine that instead of an archer our ancient Greek astronomers decided the joined-up-dots resembled my teddy bear idea, mm? That would be a whole different ball game, wouldn't it? I mean, outdoor activities? Sporty? Archery? Not typical cuddly toy mannerisms we've all grown to know and love, eh? Oh no, we'd then find Sagittarians found a whole new set of behavioural patterns thrust upon them: cuddly, docile,

I'm Not Really My Star Sign

lacking ambition etc. Which, all in all, makes something of a mockery of our associating the somewhat spurious findings of the ancient Greeks (who were well-known to have got off on all sorts of funny powders) several thousand years ago with *your* likely personality traits were you to be born during the designated Sagittarius dates. That said, it is, of course, easy to get caught up in the whole astrological way of thinking and end up getting conned into believing it. Into believing that, for instance, you're likely to share something in common with some well known, like-signed . . .

Celebrity

You know the kind of thing, 'Famous Sagittarians include: Gianni Versace, Tina Turner, Ludwig Van Beethoven etc, etc. *Wow!, you think, I'm in good company here. If these celebrated, mega-successful characters have the same star sign as yours truly there's got to be a better-than-evens chance that I'll end up on the list with them. Me, a relative nobody, all but rubbing shoulders with society's highest of high flyers.* Depending on your particular inclinations, you're about to convince yourself that you're only a stone's throw away from showing the world the real meaning of fashion, being a credible rock-septuagenarian or becoming a legendary composer. The future could hardly bode better for you. And all without any effort on your part. No, all you needed to do to qualify as one of life's true pioneers was to have planned your inaugural ETA to occur at any time between two totally inauspicious dates before hanging around for an arbitrary number of years until the relevant lumps of extra-terrestrial matter waved their magic wand in your direction. Then, hey-presto, you somehow become transmogrified into one of the chosen few. One of the special ones. An individual whose name will enjoy

I'm Not Really My Star Sign

unprecedented immortality the world over for pioneering efforts of the highest order in a chosen field of expertise. Impressive stuff, eh? Something you somehow always knew you were capable of. Something that now carries the endorsement of one of the nation's leading stargazers. It simply must be true. How can there be any doubt? Well, I'm sorry to spoil your day, pal, but things aren't quite what they seem. You see, if your friendly newspaper-oblique-periodical-oblique-TV astrologer elected, instead, to list like-sign, *non*-celebrity figures there wouldn't be enough paper in the developed world to print a

I'm Not Really My Star Sign

46

fraction of their names on. And that's because there are, very sadly, many, many times more *non* Gianni-Tina-Ludwigs on this planet than actual Gianni-Tina-Ludwigs. Honestly. You see, you'd have taken one look at the overwhelming anonymity and insignificance of the individuals listed, whose birth sign coincided with yours, before witnessing the unwelcome onset of an acute attack of terminal self-deprecation. Really. I mean, how could you possibly gain solace from the inescapable truth that Versace's little club of celebrities was comprised of no more than an infinitesimal

I'm Not Really My Star Sign

number of members whose very exclusivity defined them as positively non-Sagittarian-like? Mm? Makes sense? Of course it does. If being a Sagittarian, above all else, means being like other Sagittarians, past and present, then being a Sagittarian means, by definition, leading an existence of little or no significance. Period. I'm sorry, but it's not my fault that you're gullible enough to place your trust in some airy-fairy, self-appointed prophet who's managed to coin an enviable living, thank-you very much, by publishing or broadcasting a load of intellectually-devoid twaddle.

I'm Not Really My Star Sign

50

Celebrity

But, then again, maybe it's just me. I could be doing these people a great disservice. It might be no more than a simple matter of neurological . . .

Which would lead to me being, in a technical sense, fundamentally different to everyone else. Not capable of being a Sagittarian. Born during a Sagittarian period but, for whatever reason, not a properly developed specimen. Could be that I'm missing some vital astrological

Connections

component or other. Something that happened during the very early stages of my existence. Or even earlier: during, you know, the very event that led to my entry into the world in the first place. Like there was some incompatibility problem with my Mum and Dad's chromosomes which ended up with me not being properly equipped in the astro dept. Well, things could have been a lot worse, couldn't they? Not exactly the most debilitating congenital problem. My only hindrance was not being able to access the necessary data connect-ions. Look, I'm deadly serious here. You might have precisely what's needed to

I'm Not Really My Star Sign

Connections

log onto the stars to enjoy the whole astrological experience but for me it just doesn't happen. And, as a result, I end up being, well, critical. God, I'm no psychiatrist but I've probably got some kind of psychological, anti-astrology hang-up. Instead of adopting a more measured perspective, I find I'm inclined to view the subject with, well, contempt I suppose – don't know if that comes across in my writing. Anyway, let me give you an example – an example that might make this issue appear a little more straightforward. Right, you ready? Well, some people sign up with satellite TV providers, okay? And some people don't, yeah? Right, if you're one of the satellite TV signer-uppers you'll have a little decoding box next to your telly and a dish on the outside of the property. And inside the decoding box there's a little plastic card that holds all the information about your contract, like whether you've paid your monthly fee, what packages you subscribe to, your PIN and all other sorts of things that allow the audiovisual signals that hit the dish to make their way to the TV. Yeah, it's a bit complicated, I know, but, you see, if any of these important bits and pieces don't perform like they should you don't end up with any sound (the audio bit) or a picture (the visual bit). Follow that? Right, now on to me: imagine the three bits of satellite TV kit – the box, the dish and the plastic card – are equal to astro chromosomes. Okay, it might not be the best example but stay with me on this. Right, now consider the folk who haven't chosen to enjoy the satellite TV experience, yeah? And, also, the folk whose plastic card isn't reading right. Well, it doesn't matter how hard either of them try, or how strong their desire is, they just ain't going to be able to get the information that keeps hitting the dish onto the screen. It just ain't gonna happen. No way. So, you see, my situation

I'm Not Really My Star Sign

Connections

isn't a whole lot different: no box/dish/plastic equals no satellite progs . . . no astro components equals no zodiac experience. Get it? Something I'm going to have to live with. Got no choice. And it means that I'll just have to skip over the page when the header reads . . .

Horoscopes

Not that they hold much interest for me anyway. Can't say I've ever felt hard done-by in not being given to taking a glimpse at what's deemed to be in store for me during the course of the coming 24 hours. Always seem to get through the day without any problem. But I suppose it would be an advantage to have at least

Horoscopes

an inkling of what's likely to be round the corner. For instance, if the zodiacal-columnist lets you in on the fact that it might be preferable to hold fire on talking to your partner about some sensitive issue or other for a day or two because of your particular, personal, astro-link-up with, say, Mars, then it *would* lead to a more harmonious existence, wouldn't it. I mean, if, and only, if, these experts do know what they're talking about, when it comes to Sagittarians, advice on matters regarding their innate philosophical powers, for example, (a quality about which astrologers the

Horoscopes

world over would appear to be of one mind) will be based firmly on their knowledge of Sagittarians' proclivities in this direction. And I imagine it wouldn't be difficult for them to marry this information up with the likely disposition of other star signers (calculated, no doubt, from the day's specific star/planet/asteroid/comet distribution pattern) to decide that some domestic/financial/sexual matter, or other, will best be dealt with once the relevant heavenly bodies have managed to rearrange themselves, hopefully, by the following afternoon. But, oh I don't know, isn't this all a bit unnecessary? I

I'm Not Really My Star Sign

Horoscopes

mean, if we're talking about pre-warning Sagittarians that danger lurks ahead in the shape of partner-related, pro-sensitive mood swings then isn't this tantamount to suggesting that there's an incompatibility problem anyway? You know, between the two individuals' intrinsic star-sign characteristics? Well, there'd have to be, wouldn't there? I mean, if I'm true to the nature of my zodiac sign wouldn't I have automatically selected a companion with a complementary birth date? Like a Leonine, for instance, where it would be near on impossible for us not to bring out the best in each other and enjoy

I'm Not Really My Star Sign

a comfortable and fulfilling relationship for years. And if I hadn't, wouldn't we have realized we were unsuited at the outset? Surely, this is the basis of achieving a true bond. And without it, well, maybe a confrontation wouldn't be such a bad thing. An opportunity for both parties to expose their differences, part company and seek out like-minded mates elsewhere. Or am I missing the point here? Perhaps the real function of horoscopes is to see that astrologically-challenged folk like me are kept abreast of possible hazards on a daily basis. Hazards resulting from our not having enjoyed access to conventional

I'm Not Really My Star Sign

Horoscopes

zodiac partner selection processes. Yes, that makes a lot more sense. Perfectly formed Sagittarians have no need for horoscopes – they're simply a service dedicated to the needs of deficient numptys like me. Duh! How could I have been so dumb? If the truth be known, it probably forms part of some government health and safety policy. But the whole matter of astrological reading still seems a rather over-complicated way of attempting to predict an individual's future, don't you agree? I mean, wouldn't it be far simpler and less time-consuming to simply check out the grouts at the bottom of your teacup? All that plotting of

I'm Not Really My Star Sign

Horoscopes

stars and stuff? Seems like a lot of trouble to me. For goodness' sake, aren't tea leaves a bit more accessible than hundreds of distant stars? Stars that are light-years away from us? Stars that they reckon are directly responsible for my being inclined towards a whole variety of Sagittarian-typical...

Mmm, traits that have absolutely nothing to do with my cultural development or early childhood experiences or exposure to inspirational characters. You see, notwithstanding the role played by my particular star constellation, the principal authority responsible for shaping my personality is none other than

Traits?

the planet, Jupiter. That ginormous lump of inorganic rock 500-odd million miles away from Earth which spends its time happily floating around the sun once every 12 years. Not my Mum, not my Dad, not my teachers, not my religious leader, not my librarian, not my internet account, not my university professors, not anyone. Just a big lump of gas. They're having a laugh, aren't they? Just think, were I to have been conceived several weeks earlier, all of my particular attributes would have been, magically, inaccessible to me. Well, thank you, Mum and Dad, for getting down to it when you did. Very considerate of you because I've

I'm Not Really My Star Sign

Traits?

always wanted to be an optimistic technophile with a masculine bent. Wouldn't have been at all happy with one of those God-awful feminine, fearless, controlling Scorpio personalities. Probably would have ended up as some kind of military chief. You can just imagine the pre-coital conversation, can't you: "I say, darling, do you realise it's nearing the end of February? Might it not be an ideal time for us to start thinking about that tactless little computer programmer we've always promised ourselves? I'll clear up down here while you go upstairs to get yourself ready". Yeah? Oh, come

I'm Not Really My Star Sign

on, it just doesn't happen, does it? Knowing my Mum, Dad would have got a clump round the head. I mean, forget Huxley's *Brave New World*, this is social engineering on a serious scale. And don't you think that, if society really did recognise this astrology business as anything remotely

approaching a valid concept, life as we know it would have terminated years ago? Imagine the difference it would make to our days in the classroom for example:
Teacher: "Now look here, Smith, how many times have I told you that I will not tolerate such appallingly presented work?"
Smith: "Give me a break, Sir, you

Traits?

know full well that Jupiter just doesn't connect with your subject." Be handy, wouldn't it? And in these politically correct times, you can be sure that the European Court of Human Rights would have something to say on the matter if teacher tried to push his luck too far. Too right it would. Smith and the family lawyer would be up there in a flash if they thought they could nail something on him. But they don't do that, do they. And that's because our friend, Smithy, would be laughed out of the European Court if he so much as thought about presenting such a case. The truth is, society treats the whole thing with as much credibility

Traits? as it does the grouts in the bottom of the little old lady down the road's tea cup. And what is it with the astrologers' fixation on . . .

Constellations?

Well, honestly! I sometimes wonder if they have any comprehension of how far away these things actually are. Okay, you might be able to see them (well some of them) if you get yourself on the right end of a decent telescope, providing there's not too much cloud around but, really, these mega-normous lumps of

Constellations?

twinkling matter are a long way off. A very long way off. Like light-years off. Yes, light-years! And light can travel a few miles in a year, trust me. I mean, come on, what sort of influence can we honestly expect them to exert on us, eh? Well, we only have five senses so it doesn't take long to work out where the influence might take hold. Let's start with sight. No problem because they are almost virtually invisible to us. Hearing? Well, they're certainly not bothering me. Can anybody tell me what they sound like? Taste? Touch, Smell? Oh, come on, this is a no-brainer. So, how are we being influenced by them? And all

I'm Not Really My Star Sign

Constellations?

that bow-and-arrow symbolism stuff. What is that all about? Loads of stars floating around millions of miles away representing a centaur? Really? What were those Greek astronomers smoking for God's sake? Centaurs? Stars? Some imagination! Okay, okay I know it was a few years ago when some learned figure

I'm Not Really My Star Sign

looked up into the sky and decided there was definitely something archer-like going on up there but, please, why are we going along with it all these centuries later? Look, it might have seemed reasonable at the time, I'll grant you, but we're talking about a period in history when the brainiest, quickest-witted

Constellations?

intellectuals genuinely thought the Sun whizzed its merry way around the Earth. Which, don't misunderstand me, I'm not suggesting was stupid. No, definitely not. I doubt many of us would have thought any differently had we, ourselves, been living in those times. But today's astrologers aren't living in those times, are they? So why do they still follow their out-dated wisdom? Seems totally nuts to me. Look, we know a lot more about the Universe these days and are far more aware of the scale of things. And the number of heavenly bodies up there. And down there, come to that. So consider this:

I'm Not Really My Star Sign

Constellations?

what relevance would the apparent proximity of the archer-depicting Sagittarius stars have were they to be viewed, or photographed, even, from an alternative vantage point in the Universe? Now don't be a smarty pants, I know it isn't possible if you're human but, in theory, yeah? What would our beautiful archer shapes look like then? Yes, right, nothing like archers at all because you couldn't even capture the Sagittarius stars in the same view. Not even with the very latest hi-tech, ultra-wide-angled, super-fisheye, twenty-mega pixel, Leiconblad. No, not even with one of those. And why is that? Mm? I mean,

I'm Not Really My Star Sign

Constellations?

hello . . is anyone at home? . . . parallax? Ever heard of that? Blimey, you couldn't make it up, could you? Parallax, I'm sorry to inform you, would render our lovely little archery pattern (which, actually, looks nothing like an archery pattern, anyway) of no consequence whatsoever if viewed from anywhere but planet Earth. My apologies for delivering this bombshell but I'm afraid, no matter how unromantic it might sound, none of the stars in any of our beautifully-fabricated constellations bears any special relationship, whatsoever, with any of the others. Nothing at all. Zero.

I'm Not Really My Star Sign

Constellations?

Zilch. Nil. Nought. Get it? Nothing. They simply don't have any more to do with each other than they do with any of the other stars. So could somebody please bring our dear little astrological friends up to date – into the twenty-first century – so that we can be done with all this silly constellation nonsense. Am I

I'm Not Really My Star Sign

really a Sagittarian? No, of course I'm not, and neither is anyone else. Anyway, if you'll kindly excuse me, sitting here all day plays havoc with my sciatica – must take a stretch.